The Genie

A play by Julia Donaldson

Illustrated by Shahab Shamshirsaz

Characters

Mum: That was a nice picnic.

Dad: I think I'll have a little nap.

Samson: Woof! Woof!

Adam: Are there any more crisps? Samson wants some.

Emily: No, you gave the last packet to him, remember?

Adam: I did not!

Emily: Yes you did!

Mum: Stop squabbling, you two.

Dad: Why don't you go for a paddle?

Emily: No – it's too cold.

Adam: I know! Let's throw some sticks for Samson. Here you are, boy!

He throws a stick into the sea.

Samson: Woof! Woof!

He fetches the stick.

Emily: Ow! He splashed me! The water's freezing!

Samson: Woof, woof! Woof, woof!

Emily: Why is he barking so much?

Adam: He's seen something in the water. What is it, Samson?

Emily: Look, it's a bottle.

Adam: I'll see if I can reach it with this stick.

Emily: It's got a cork in it.

Adam: It looks very old.

Genie: Let me out! Let me out!

Emily: Did you hear that?

Adam: There's something in the bottle.

Emily: Or someone!

Genie: Let me out! Let me out!

Samson: Woof, woof!

Adam: Mum! Dad! Have you got a corkscrew?

Mum: I think there's one in the picnic basket.

Dad: Yes. Here it is.

He opens the bottle.

Genie: Thank you!

Mum: Who are you?

Genie: I'm a genie, and you've just rescued me. Now I can grant you three wishes.

Emily: But there are four of us!

Genie: Oh, all right then – four wishes. But that's my limit.

Adam: I wish my dog could talk.

Genie: Hey presto!

Samson: Hi, Adam! Are you going to throw me another stick?

Adam: Amazing! My wish has come true.

Genie: It's not amazing at all.

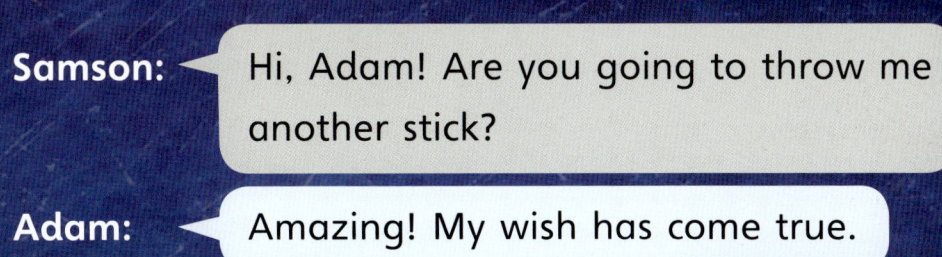

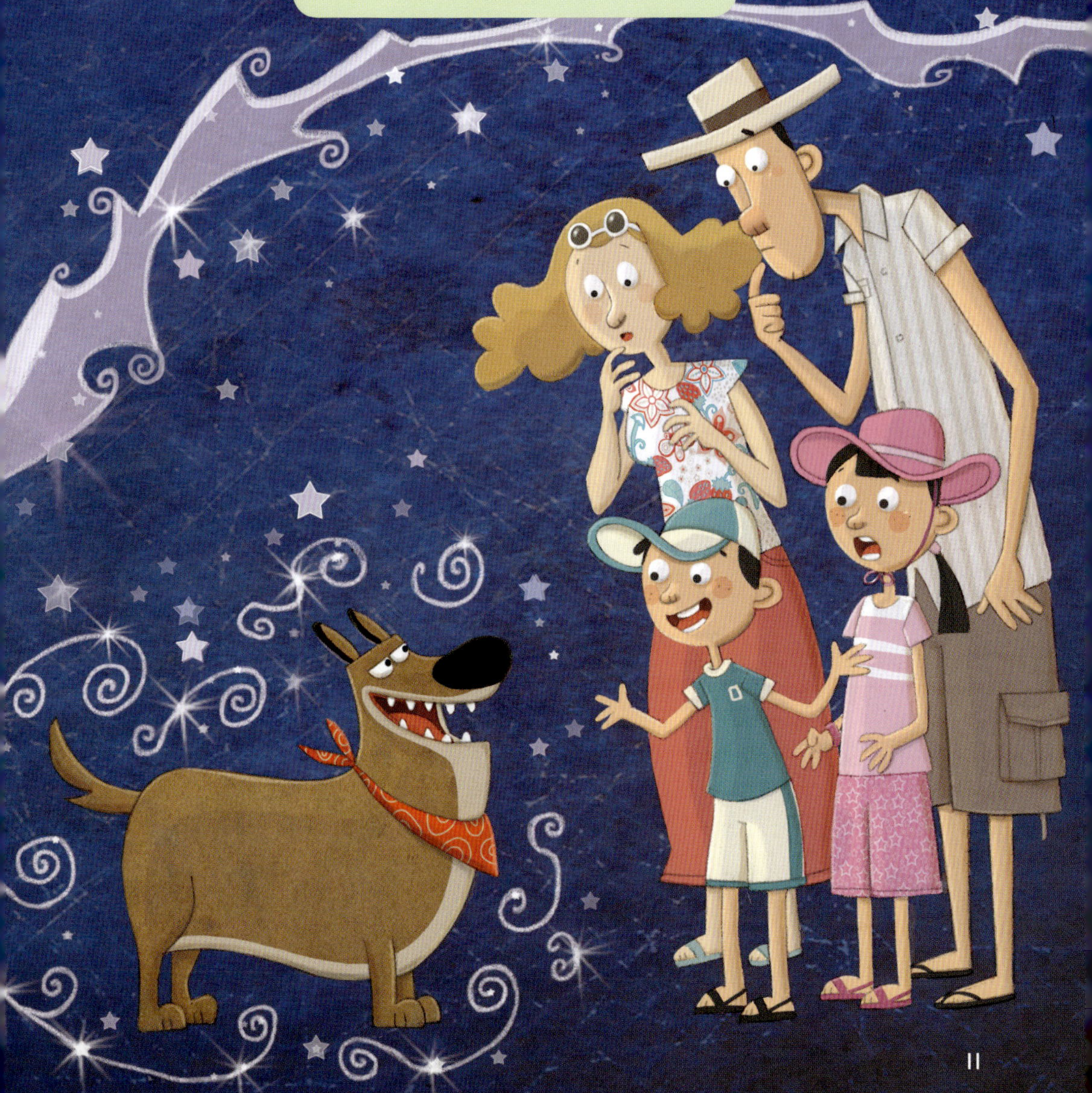

Samson: Stop chatting, you two. Throw that stick, Adam!

Adam: You love sticks, don't you?

Samson: Yes! I wish you did too. You would if you were a dog like me.

Genie: Hey presto!

Adam turns into a dog.

Mum: What's happening?

Dad: Adam has turned into a dog!

Mum: Oh no! This is terrible!

Emily: Can you talk, Adam?

Adam: Woof, woof!

Dad: He's trying to say "Change me back into a boy."

Samson: No he's not. He's saying "Throw a stick."

Genie: Now you only have two wishes left.

Emily: That's not fair. You weren't supposed to give a wish to the dog!

Genie: Oh, all right then – three more wishes, but that's my limit. One for the girl, and one each for the grown-ups.

Mum: Well, I know what my wish is. Turn that dog back into a boy!

Genie: You want me to turn this dog into a boy?

Mum: Yes.

Genie: Hey presto!

Samson turns into a boy.

Dad: No, not that dog – the other one!

Emily: Too late! Now Samson has turned into a boy!

Mum: And Adam is still a dog.

Adam: Woof, woof!

Mum: Oh no!

Genie: Some people are never happy.

Samson: Cheer up – at least you've got two wishes left.

Emily: Yes – and I know what I want. A pony!

Genie: Hey presto!

A pony appears.

Emily: Oh look! Isn't he beautiful!

Mum: Really, Emily! You should have wished for your brother back.

Emily: Why? I think I prefer having Samson as my brother.

Adam: Woof, woof!

Samson: He wants a stick. Here you are, Adam!

He throws a stick and Adam fetches it.

Genie: Just one wish left now.

Dad: Yes, and it's mine.

Mum: But we can help you decide what to wish for.

Emily: I think he should wish that my pony could talk.

Dad: No way!

Samson: I think he should wish for another dog. I was quite lonely when I was a dog and there was only one of me.

Mum: Don't be silly. He should wish for Adam to turn back into a boy and for Samson to turn back into a dog.

Genie: But that's two wishes. I can't do that.

Adam: Woof, woof! Woof, woof!

Dad: Why is Adam barking so much?

Samson: He just wants another stick.

Emily: No – I think he's trying to tell Dad what to wish for.

Mum: Look, he's scratching in the sand with his paw.

Dad: Yes, he's writing something.

Samson: What does it say? I can't read.

Emily: It says, "Put the clock back."

Mum: Of course! That's a good idea.

Emily: I don't understand.

Dad: I do. Listen to me, Genie. I wish to put the clock back to before the children found the bottle.

Genie: Oh no! Are you sure that's what you want?

Dad: Yes, quite sure.

Emily: But then I'll lose my pony!

Genie: Too bad! Hey presto!

The genie and the pony disappear. Adam turns back into a boy and Samson turns back into a dog.

Mum: Well, that was a nice picnic.

Dad: I think I'll have a little nap.

Samson: Woof! Woof!

Adam: Samson wants a stick. Here you are, boy!

He throws a stick into the sea. Samson fetches it.

Emily: Ow! He splashed me! The water's freezing!

Samson: Woof, woof! Woof, woof!

Adam: He's seen something in the water. What is it, Samson?

Emily: Look, it's a bottle!

Genie: Let me out! Let me out!

Adam: Do you think we should?